Life Is A Dream

by:
Pedro Calderon de la Barca

Paperback: 978-939-1560-50-8

Any references to historical events, real people, or real places are used fictitiously. Names, characters, and places are products of the author's imagination.

sanagepublishing@gmail.com

Designed by:
allpublishingsolution.com

CONTENTS

Introductory note 1

Life is a dream 3

Act I 4

Act II 38

Act III 72

Act IV 98

INTRODUCTORY NOTE

Pedro Calderon de la Barca was born in Madrid, January 17, 1600, of good family. He was educated at the Jesuit College in Madrid and at the University of Salamanca; and a doubtful tradition says that he began to write plays at the age of thirteen. His literary activity was interrupted for ten years, 1625-1635, by military service in Italy and the Low Countries, and again for a year or more in Catalonia. In 1637 he became a Knight of the Order of Santiago, and in 1651 he entered the priesthood, rising to the dignity of Superior of the Brotherhood of San Pedro in Madrid. He held various offices in the court of Philip IV, who rewarded his services with pensions, and had his plays produced with great splendor. He died May 5, 1681.

At the time when Calderon began to compose for the stage, the Spanish drama was at its height. Lope de Vega, the most prolific and, with Calderon, the greatest, of Spanish dramatists, was still alive; and by his applause gave encouragement to the beginner whose fame was to rival his own. The national type of drama which Lope had established was maintained in its essential characteristics by Calderon, and he produced abundant specimens of all its varieties. Of regular plays he has left a hundred and twenty; of "Autos Sacramentales," the peculiar Spanish allegorical development of the medieval mystery, we have seventy-three; besides a considerable number of farces.

The dominant motives in Calderon's dramas are characteristically national: fervid loyalty to Church and King, and a sense of honor heightened almost to the point of the fantastic. Though his plays are laid in a great variety of scenes and ages, the sentiment and the characters remain essentially Spanish; and this intensely local quality has probably lessened the vogue of Calderon in other countries. In the construction and conduct of his plots he showed great skill, yet the ingenuity expended in the management of the story did not restrain the fiery emotion and opulent imagination which mark his finest speeches and give them a lyric quality which some critics regard as his greatest distinction.

Of all Calderon's works, "Life is a Dream" may be regarded as the most universal in its theme. It seeks to teach a lesson that may be learned from the philosophers and religious thinkers of many ages—that the world of our senses is a mere shadow, and that the only reality is to be found in the invisible and eternal. The story which forms its basis is Oriental in origin, and in the form of the legend of "Barlaam and Josaphat" was familiar in all the literatures of the Middle Ages. Combined with this in the plot is the tale of Abou Hassan from the "Arabian Nights," the main situations in which are turned to farcical purposes in the Induction to the Shakespearean "Taming of the Shrew." But with Calderon the theme is lifted altogether out of the atmosphere of comedy, and is worked up with poetic sentiment and a touch of mysticism into a symbolic drama of profound and universal philosophical significance.

LIFE IS A DREAM

Dramatis Personae

Basilio	King of Poland.
Segismund	his Son.
Astolfo	his Nephew.
Estrella	his Niece.
Clotaldo	a General in Basilio's Service.
Rosaura	a Muscovite Lady.
Fife	her Attendant.

Chamberlain, Lords in Waiting, Officers, Soldiers, etc., in Basilio's Service.

The Scene of the first and third Acts lies on the Polish frontier: of the second Act, in Warsaw.

As this version of Calderon's drama is not for acting, a higher and wider mountain-scene than practicable may be imagined for Rosaura's descent in the first Act and the soldiers' ascent in the last. The bad watch kept by the sentinels who guarded their state-prisoner, together with much else (not all!) that defies sober sense in this wild drama, I must leave Calderon to answer for; whose audience were not critical of detail and probability, so long as a good story, with strong, rapid, and picturesque action and situation, was set before them.

ACT 1

SCENE I—A pass of rocks, over which a storm is rolling away, and the sun setting: in the foreground, half- way down, a fortress.

(Enter first from the topmost rock Rosaura, as from horseback, in man's attire; and, after her, Fife.)

ROSAURA.
There, four-footed Fury, blast
Engender'd brute, without the wit
Of brute, or mouth to match the bit
Of man—art satisfied at last?
Who, when thunder roll'd aloof,
Tow'rd the spheres of fire your ears
Pricking, and the granite kicking
Into lightning with your hoof,
Among the tempest-shatter'd crags
Shattering your luckless rider
Back into the tempest pass'd?
There then lie to starve and die,
Or find another Phaeton
Mad-mettled as yourself; for I,
Wearied, worried, and for-done,
Alone will down the mountain try,
That knits his brows against the sun.

FIFE (as to his mule).
There, thou mis-begotten thing,
Long-ear'd lightning, tail'd tornado,
Griffin-hoof-in hurricano,
(I might swear till I were almost
Hoarse with roaring Asonante)
Who forsooth because our betters
Would begin to kick and fling
You forthwith your noble mind
Must prove, and kick me off behind,
Tow'rd the very centre whither
Gravity was most inclined.
There where you have made your bed
In it lie; for, wet or dry,
Let what will for me betide you,
Burning, blowing, freezing, hailing;
Famine waste you: devil ride you:
Tempest baste you black and blue:
(To Rosaura.)
There! I think in downright railing
I can hold my own with you.

ROS.
Ah, my good Fife, whose merry loyal pipe,
Come weal, come woe, is never out of tune
What, you in the same plight too?

FIFE.
Ay; And madam—sir—hereby desire,
When you your own adventures sing
Another time in lofty rhyme,
You don't forget the trusty squire

Who went with you Don-quixoting.

ROS.
Well, my good fellow—to leave Pegasus
Who scarce can serve us than our horses worse—
They say no one should rob another of
The single satisfaction he has left
Of singing his own sorrows; one so great,
So says some great philosopher, that trouble
Were worth encount'ring only for the sake
Of weeping over—what perhaps you know
Some poet calls the 'luxury of woe.'

FIFE.
Had I the poet or philosopher
In the place of her that kick'd me off to ride,
I'd test his theory upon his hide.
But no bones broken, madam—sir, I mean?—

ROS.
A scratch here that a handkerchief will heal—
And you?—

FIFE.
A scratch in quiddity, or kind:
But not in 'quo'—my wounds are all behind.
But, as you say, to stop this strain,
Which, somehow, once one's in the vein,
Comes clattering after—there again!—
What are we twain—deuce take't!—we two,
I mean, to do—drench'd through and through—
Oh, I shall choke of rhymes, which I believe

Are all that we shall have to live on here.

ROS.
What, is our victual gone too?—

FIFE.
Ay, that brute
Has carried all we had away with her,
Clothing, and cate, and all.

ROS.
And now the sun,
Our only friend and guide, about to sink
Under the stage of earth.

FIFE.
And enter Night,
With Capa y Espada—and—pray heaven!
With but her lanthorn also.

ROS.
Ah, I doubt
To-night, if any, with a dark one—or
Almost burnt out after a month's consumption.
Well! well or ill, on horseback or afoot,
This is the gate that lets me into Poland;
And, sorry welcome as she gives a guest
Who writes his own arrival on her rocks
In his own blood—
Yet better on her stony threshold die,
Than live on unrevenged in Muscovy.

FIFE.
Oh, what a soul some women have—I mean
Some men—
Oh, Fife, Fife, as you love me, Fife,
Make yourself perfect in that little part,
Or all will go to ruin!

FIFE.
Oh, I will,
Please God we find some one to try it on.
But, truly, would not any one believe
Some fairy had exchanged us as we lay
Two tiny foster-children in one cradle?

ROS.
Well, be that as it may, Fife, it reminds me
Of what perhaps I should have thought before,
But better late than never—You know I love you,
As you, I know, love me, and loyally
Have follow'd me thus far in my wild venture.
Well! now then—having seen me safe thus far
Safe if not wholly sound—over the rocks
Into the country where my business lies
Why should not you return the way we came,
The storm all clear'd away, and, leaving me
(Who now shall want you, though not thank you, less,
Now that our horses gone) this side the ridge,
Find your way back to dear old home again;
While I—Come, come!—
What, weeping my poor fellow?

FIFE.
Leave you here

Alone—my Lady—Lord! I mean my Lord—
In a strange country—among savages—
Oh, now I know—you would be rid of me
For fear my stumbling speech—

ROS.
Oh, no, no, no!—
I want you with me for a thousand sakes
To which that is as nothing—I myself
More apt to let the secret out myself
Without your help at all—Come, come, cheer up!
And if you sing again, 'Come weal, come woe,'
Let it be that; for we will never part
Until you give the signal.

FIFE.
'Tis a bargain.

ROS.
Now to begin, then. 'Follow, follow me,
'You fairy elves that be.'

FIFE.
Ay, and go on—
Something of 'following darkness like a dream,'
For that we're after.
No, after the sun;
Trying to catch hold of his glittering skirts
That hang upon the mountain as he goes.

FIFE.
Ah, he's himself past catching—as you spoke
He heard what you were saying, and—just so—

Like some scared water-bird,
As we say in my country, dove below.

ROS.
Well, we must follow him as best we may.
Poland is no great country, and, as rich
In men and means, will but few acres spare
To lie beneath her barrier mountains bare.
We cannot, I believe, be very far
From mankind or their dwellings.

FIFE.
Send it so!
And well provided for man, woman, and beast.
No, not for beast. Ah, but my heart begins
To yearn for her—

ROS.
Keep close, and keep your feet
From serving you as hers did.

FIFE.
As for beasts,
If in default of other entertainment,
We should provide them with ourselves to eat—
Bears, lions, wolves—

ROS.
Oh, never fear.

FIFE.
Or else,
Default of other beasts, beastlier men,

Cannibals, Anthropophagi, bare Poles
Who never knew a tailor but by taste.

ROS.
Look, look! Unless my fancy misconceive
With twilight—down among the rocks there,
Fife— Some human dwelling, surely—
Or think you but a rock torn from the rocks
In some convulsion like to-day's, and perch'd
Quaintly among them in mock-masonry?

FIFE.
Most likely that, I doubt.

ROS.
No, no—for look!
A square of darkness opening in it—

FIFE.
Oh, I don't half like such openings!—

ROS.
Like the loom
Of night from which she spins her outer gloom—

FIFE.
Lord, Madam, pray forbear this tragic vein
In such a time and place—

ROS.
And now again
Within that square of darkness, look! a light
That feels its way with hesitating pulse,

As we do, through the darkness that it drives
To blacken into deeper night beyond.

FIFE.
In which could we follow that light's example,
As might some English Bardolph with his nose,
We might defy the sunset—Hark, a chain!

ROS.
And now a lamp, a lamp! And now the hand
That carries it.

FIFE.
Oh, Lord! that dreadful chain!

ROS.
And now the bearer of the lamp; indeed
As strange as any in Arabian tale,
So giant-like, and terrible, and grand,
Spite of the skin he's wrapt in.

FIFE.
Why, 'tis his own:
Oh, 'tis some wild man of the woods; I've heard
They build and carry torches—

ROS.
Never Ape
Bore such a brow before the heavens as that—
Chain'd as you say too!—

FIFE.
Oh, that dreadful chain!

ROS.
And now he sets the lamp down by his side,
And with one hand clench'd in his tangled hair
And with a sigh as if his heart would break—

(During this Segismund has entered from the fortress, with a torch.)

SEGISMUND.
Once more the storm has roar'd itself away,
Splitting the crags of God as it retires;
But sparing still what it should only blast,
This guilty piece of human handiwork,
And all that are within it. Oh, how oft,
How oft, within or here abroad, have
I Waited, and in the whisper of my heart
Pray'd for the slanting hand of heaven to strike
The blow myself I dared not, out of fear
Of that Hereafter, worse, they say, than here,
Plunged headlong in, but, till dismissal waited,
To wipe at last all sorrow from men's eyes,
And make this heavy dispensation clear.
Thus have I borne till now, and still endure,
Crouching in sullen impotence day by day,
Till some such out-burst of the elements
Like this rouses the sleeping fire within;
And standing thus upon the threshold of
Another night about to close the door
Upon one wretched day to open it
On one yet wretcheder because one more;—
Once more, you savage heavens, I ask of you—
I, looking up to those relentless eyes
That, now the greater lamp is gone below,

Begin to muster in the listening skies;
In all the shining circuits you have gone
About this theatre of human woe,
What greater sorrow have you gazed upon
Than down this narrow chink you witness still;
And which, did you yourselves not fore-devise,
You registered for others to fulfil!

FIFE.
This is some Laureate at a birthday ode;
No wonder we went rhyming.

ROS.
Hush! And now
See, starting to his feet, he strides about
Far as his tether'd steps—

SEG.
And if the chain
You help'd to rivet round me did contract
Since guiltless infancy from guilt in act;
Of what in aspiration or in thought
Guilty, but in resentment of the wrong
That wreaks revenge on wrong I never wrought
By excommunication from the free
Inheritance that all created life,
Beside myself, is born to—from the wings
That range your own immeasurable blue,
Down to the poor, mute, scale-imprison'd things,
That yet are free to wander, glide, and pass
About that under-sapphire, whereinto
Yourselves transfusing you yourselves englass!

ROS.
What mystery is this?

FIFE.
Why, the man's mad:
That's all the mystery. That's why he's chain'd—
And why—

SEG.
Nor Nature's guiltless life alone—
But that which lives on blood and rapine; nay,
Charter'd with larger liberty to slay
Their guiltless kind, the tyrants of the air
Soar zenith-upward with their screaming prey,
Making pure heaven drop blood upon the stage
Of under earth, where lion, wolf, and bear,
And they that on their treacherous velvet wear
Figure and constellation like your own,
With their still living slaughter bound away
Over the barriers of the mountain cage,
Against which one, blood-guiltless, and endued
With aspiration and with aptitude
Transcending other creatures, day by day
Beats himself mad with unavailing rage!

FIFE.
Why, that must be the meaning of my mule's
Rebellion—

ROS.
Hush!

SEG.
But then if murder be
The law by which not only conscience-blind
Creatures, but man too prospers with his kind;
Who leaving all his guilty fellows free,
Under your fatal auspice and divine
Compulsion, leagued in some mysterious ban
Against one innocent and helpless man,
Abuse their liberty to murder mine:
And sworn to silence, like their masters mute
In heaven, and like them twirling through the mask
Of darkness, answering to all I ask,
Point up to them whose work they execute!

ROS.
Ev'n as I thought, some poor unhappy wretch,
By man wrong'd, wretched, unrevenged, as I!
Nay, so much worse than I, as by those chains
Clipt of the means of self-revenge on those
Who lay on him what they deserve. And I,
Who taunted Heaven a little while ago
With pouring all its wrath upon my head—
Alas! like him who caught the cast-off husk
Of what another bragg'd of feeding on,
Here's one that from the refuse of my sorrows
Could gather all the banquet he desires!
Poor soul, poor soul!

FIFE.
Speak lower—he will hear you.

ROS.
And if he should, what then? Why, if he would,

He could not harm me—Nay, and if he could,
Methinks I'd venture something of a life
I care so little for—

SEG.
Who's that? Clotaldo? Who are you, I say,
That, venturing in these forbidden rocks,
Have lighted on my miserable life,
And your own death?

ROS.
You would not hurt me, surely?

SEG.
Not I; but those that, iron as the chain
In which they slay me with a lingering death,
Will slay you with a sudden—Who are you?

ROS.
A stranger from across the mountain there,
Who, having lost his way in this strange land
And coming night, drew hither to what seem'd
A human dwelling hidden in these rocks,
And where the voice of human sorrow soon
Told him it was so.

SEG.
Ay? But nearer—nearer—
That by this smoky supplement of day
But for a moment I may see who speaks
So pitifully sweet.

FIFE.
Take care! take care!

ROS.
Alas, poor man, that I, myself so helpless,
Could better help you than by barren pity,
And my poor presence—

SEG.
Oh, might that be all!
But that—a few poor moments—and, alas!
The very bliss of having, and the dread
Of losing, under such a penalty
As every moment's having runs more near,
Stifles the very utterance and resource
They cry for quickest; till from sheer despair
Of holding thee, methinks myself would tear
To pieces—

FIFE.
There, his word's enough for it.

SEG.
Oh, think, if you who move about at will,
And live in sweet communion with your kind,
After an hour lost in these lonely rocks
Hunger and thirst after some human voice
To drink, and human face to feed upon;
What must one do where all is mute, or harsh,
And ev'n the naked face of cruelty
Were better than the mask it works beneath?—
Across the mountain then! Across the mountain!
What if the next world which they tell one of

Be only next across the mountain then,
Though I must never see it till I die,
And you one of its angels?

ROS.
Alas; alas!
No angel! And the face you think so fair,
'Tis but the dismal frame-work of these rocks
That makes it seem so; and the world I come from—
Alas, alas, too many faces there
Are but fair vizors to black hearts below,
Or only serve to bring the wearer woe!
But to yourself—If haply the redress
That I am here upon may help to yours.
I heard you tax the heavens with ordering,
And men for executing, what, alas!
I now behold. But why, and who they are
Who do, and you who suffer—

SEG. (pointing upwards). Ask of them,
Whom, as to-night, I have so often ask'd,
And ask'd in vain.

ROS.
But surely, surely—

SEG.
Hark!
The trumpet of the watch to shut us in.
Oh, should they find you!—Quick!
Behind the rocks! To-morrow—if to-morrow—

ROS. (flinging her sword toward him).

Take my sword!
(Rosaura and Fife hide in the rocks; Enter Clotaldo)

CLOTALDO.
These stormy days you like to see the last of
Are but ill opiates, Segismund, I think,
For night to follow: and to-night you seem
More than your wont disorder'd. What!
A sword? Within there!
(Enter Soldiers with black vizors and torches)

FIFE.
Here's a pleasant masquerade!

CLO.
Whosever watch this was
Will have to pay head-reckoning. Meanwhile,
This weapon had a wearer. Bring him here,
Alive or dead.

SEG.
Clotaldo! good Clotaldo!—

CLO. (to Soldiers who enclose Segismund; others searching the rocks).
You know your duty.

SOLDIERS (bringing in Rosaura and Fife).
Here are two of them,
Whoever more to follow—

CLO.
Who are you,

That in defiance of known proclamation
Are found, at night-fall too, about this place?

FIFE.
Oh, my Lord, she—I mean he—

ROS.
Silence, Fife,
And let me speak for both.—Two foreign men,
To whom your country and its proclamations
Are equally unknown; and had we known,
Ourselves not masters of our lawless beasts
That, terrified by the storm among your rocks,
Flung us upon them to our cost.

FIFE.
My mule—

CLO.
Foreigners? Of what country?

ROS.
Muscovy.

CLO.
And whither bound?

ROS.
Hither—if this be Poland;
But with no ill design on her, and therefore
Taking it ill that we should thus be stopt
Upon her threshold so uncivilly.

CLO.
Whither in Poland?

ROS.
To the capital.

CLO.
And on what errand?

ROS.
Set me on the road,
And you shall be the nearer to my answer.

CLO. (aside).
So resolute and ready to reply,
And yet so young—and—
(Aloud.)
Well,—
Your business was not surely with the man
We found you with?

ROS.
He was the first we saw,—
And strangers and benighted, as we were,
As you too would have done in a like case,
Accosted him at once.

CLO.
Ay, but this sword?

ROS.
I flung it toward him.

CLO.
Well, and why?

ROS.
And why? But to revenge himself on those who thus
Injuriously misuse him.

CLO.
So—so—so!
'Tis well such resolution wants a beard
And, I suppose, is never to attain one.
Well, I must take you both, you and your sword,
Prisoners.

FIFE. (offering a cudgel).
Pray take mine, and welcome, sir;
I'm sure I gave it to that mule of mine
To mighty little purpose.

ROS.
Mine you have;
And may it win us some more kindliness
Than we have met with yet.

CLO (examining the sword).
More mystery!
How came you by this weapon?

ROS.
From my father.

CLO.
And do you know whence he?

ROS.
Oh, very well:
From one of this same Polish realm of yours,
Who promised a return, should come the chance,
Of courtesies that he received himself
In Muscovy, and left this pledge of it—
Not likely yet, it seems, to be redeem'd.

CLO (aside).
Oh, wondrous chance—or wondrous Providence!
The sword that I myself in Muscovy,
When these white hairs were black, for keepsake left
Of obligation for a like return
To him who saved me wounded as I lay
Fighting against his country; took me home;
Tended me like a brother till recover'd,
Perchance to fight against him once again
And now my sword put back into my hand
By his—if not his son—still, as so seeming,
By me, as first devoir of gratitude,
To seem believing, till the wearer's self
See fit to drop the ill-dissembling mask. (Aloud.)
Well, a strange turn of fortune has arrested
The sharp and sudden penalty that else
Had visited your rashness or mischance:
In part, your tender youth too—pardon me,
And touch not where your sword is not to answer—
Commends you to my care; not your life only,
Else by this misadventure forfeited;
But ev'n your errand, which, by happy chance,
Chimes with the very business I am on,
And calls me to the very point you aim at.

ROS.
The capital?

CLO.
Ay, the capital; and ev'n
That capital of capitals, the Court:
Where you may plead, and, I may promise, win
Pardon for this, you say unwilling, trespass,
And prosecute what else you have at heart,
With me to help you forward all I can;
Provided all in loyalty to those
To whom by natural allegiance I first am bound to.

ROS.
As you make, I take
Your offer: with like promise on my side
Of loyalty to you and those you serve,
Under like reservation for regards
Nearer and dearer still.

CLO.
Enough, enough;
Your hand; a bargain on both sides. Meanwhile,
Here shall you rest to-night. The break of day
Shall see us both together on the way.

ROS.
Thus then what I for misadventure blamed,
Directly draws me where my wishes aim'd.

(Exeunt.)

SCENE II.—The Palace at Warsaw

Enter on one side Astolfo, Duke of Muscovy, with his train: and, on the other, the Princess Estrella, with hers.

ASTOLFO.
My royal cousin, if so near in blood,
Till this auspicious meeting scarcely known,
Till all that beauty promised in the bud
Is now to its consummate blossom blown,
Well met at last; and may—

ESTRELLA.
Enough, my Lord,
Of compliment devised for you by some
Court tailor, and, believe me, still too short
To cover the designful heart below.

AST.
Nay, but indeed, fair cousin—

EST.
Ay, let Deed
Measure your words, indeed your flowers of speech
Ill with your iron equipage atone;
Irony indeed, and wordy compliment.

AST.
Indeed, indeed, you wrong me, royal cousin,
And fair as royal, misinterpreting
What, even for the end you think I aim at,

If false to you, were fatal to myself.

EST.
Why, what else means the glittering steel, my Lord,
That bristles in the rear of these fine words?
What can it mean, but, failing to cajole,
To fight or force me from my just pretension?

AST.
Nay, might I not ask ev'n the same of you,
The nodding helmets of whose men-at-arms
Out-crest the plumage of your lady court?

EST.
But to defend what yours would force from me.

AST.
Might not I, lady, say the same of mine?
But not to come to battle, ev'n of words,
With a fair lady, and my kinswoman;
And as averse to stand before your face,
Defenceless, and condemn'd in your disgrace,
Till the good king be here to clear it all—
Will you vouchsafe to hear me?

EST.
As you will.

AST.
You know that, when about to leave this world,
Our royal grandsire, King Alfonso, left
Three children; one a son, Basilio,
Who wears—long may he wear! the crown of Poland;

And daughters twain: of whom the elder was
Your mother, Clorilena, now some while
Exalted to a more than mortal throne;
And Recisunda, mine, the younger sister,
Who, married to the Prince of Muscovy,
Gave me the light which may she live to see
Herself for many, many years to come.
Meanwhile, good King Basilio, as you know,
Deep in abstruser studies than this world,
And busier with the stars than lady's eyes,
Has never by a second marriage yet
Replaced, as Poland ask'd of him, the heir
An early marriage brought and took away;
His young queen dying with the son she bore him;
And in such alienation grown so old
As leaves no other hope of heir to Poland
Than his two sisters' children; you, fair cousin,
And me; for whom the Commons of the realm
Divide themselves into two several factions;
Whether for you, the elder sister's child;
Or me, born of the younger, but, they say,
My natural prerogative of man
Outweighing your priority of birth.
Which discord growing loud and dangerous,
Our uncle, King Basilio, doubly sage
In prophesying and providing for
The future, as to deal with it when come,
Bids us here meet to-day in solemn council
Our several pretensions to compose.
And, but the martial out-burst that proclaims
His coming, makes all further parley vain,
Unless my bosom, by which only wise
I prophesy, now wrongly prophesies,

By such a happy compact as I dare
But glance at till the Royal Sage declare.
(Trumpets, etc. Enter King Basilio with his Council.)

ALL.
The King! God save the King!

ESTRELLA (Kneeling.)
Oh, Royal Sir!—

ASTOLFO (Kneeling.)
God save your Majesty—

KING.
Rise both of you,
Rise to my arms, Astolfo and Estrella;
As my two sisters' children always mine,
Now more than ever, since myself and Poland
Solely to you for our succession look'd.
And now give ear, you and your several factions,
And you, the Peers and Princes of this realm,
While I reveal the purport of this meeting
In words whose necessary length I trust
No unsuccessful issue shall excuse.
You and the world who have surnamed me "Sage"
Know that I owe that title, if my due,
To my long meditation on the book
Which ever lying open overhead—
The book of heaven, I mean—so few have read;
Whose golden letters on whose sapphire leaf,
Distinguishing the page of day and night,
And all the revolution of the year;
So with the turning volume where they lie

Still changing their prophetic syllables,
They register the destinies of men:
Until with eyes that, dim with years indeed,
Are quicker to pursue the stars than rule them,
I get the start of Time, and from his hand
The wand of tardy revelation draw.
Oh, had the self-same heaven upon his page
Inscribed my death ere I should read my life
And, by fore-casting of my own mischance,
Play not the victim but the suicide
In my own tragedy!—But you shall hear.
You know how once, as kings must for their people,
And only once, as wise men for themselves,
I woo'd and wedded: know too that my
Queen In childing died; but not, as you believe,
With her, the son she died in giving life to.
For, as the hour of birth was on the stroke,
Her brain conceiving with her womb, she dream'd
A serpent tore her entrail. And too surely
(For evil omen seldom speaks in vain)
The man-child breaking from that living tomb
That makes our birth the antitype of death,
Man-grateful, for the life she gave him paid
By killing her: and with such circumstance
As suited such unnatural tragedy;
He coming into light, if light it were
That darken'd at his very horoscope,
When heaven's two champions—sun and moon
I mean— Suffused in blood upon each other fell
In such a raging duel of eclipse
As hath not terrified the universe
Since that which wept in blood the death of Christ:
When the dead walk'd, the waters turn'd to blood,

Earth and her cities totter'd, and the world
Seem'd shaken to its last paralysis.
In such a paroxysm of dissolution
That son of mine was born; by that first act
Heading the monstrous catalogue of crime,
I found fore-written in his horoscope;
As great a monster in man's history
As was in nature his nativity;
So savage, bloody, terrible, and impious,
Who, should he live, would tear his country's entrails,
As by his birth his mother's; with which crime
Beginning, he should clench the dreadful tale
By trampling on his father's silver head.
All which fore-reading, and his act of birth
Fate's warrant that I read his life aright;
To save his country from his mother's fate,
I gave abroad that he had died with her
His being slew; with midnight secrecy
I had him carried to a lonely tower
Hewn from the mountain-barriers of the realm,
And under strict anathema of death
Guarded from men's inquisitive approach,
Save from the trusty few one needs must trust;
Who while his fasten'd body they provide
With salutary garb and nourishment,
Instruct his soul in what no soul may miss
Of holy faith, and in such other lore
As may solace his life-imprisonment,
And tame perhaps the Savage prophesied
Toward such a trial as I aim at now,
And now demand your special hearing to.
What in this fearful business I have done,
Judge whether lightly or maliciously,—

I, with my own and only flesh and blood,
And proper lineal inheritor!
I swear, had his foretold atrocities
Touch'd me alone. I had not saved myself
At such a cost to him; but as a king,—
A Christian king,—I say, advisedly,
Who would devote his people to a tyrant
Worse than Caligula fore-chronicled?
But even this not without grave mis-giving,
Lest by some chance mis-reading of the stars,
Or mis-direction of what rightly read,
I wrong my son of his prerogative,
And Poland of her rightful sovereign.
For, sure and certain prophets as the stars,
Although they err not, he who reads them may;
Or rightly reading—seeing there is One
Who governs them, as, under Him, they us,
We are not sure if the rough diagram
They draw in heaven and we interpret here,
Be sure of operation, if the Will
Supreme, that sometimes for some special end
The course of providential nature breaks
By miracle, may not of these same stars
ancel his own first draft, or overrule
What else fore-written all else overrules.
As, for example, should the Will Almighty
Permit the Free-will of particular man
To break the meshes of else strangling fate—
Which Free-will, fearful of foretold abuse,
I have myself from my own son fore-closed
From ever possible self-extrication;
A terrible responsibility,
Not to the conscience to be reconciled

Unless opposing almost certain evil
Against so slight contingency of good.
Well—thus perplex'd, I have resolved at last
To bring the thing to trial: whereunto
Here have I summon'd you, my Peers, and you
Whom I more dearly look to, failing him,
As witnesses to that which I propose;
And thus propose the doing it. Clotaldo,
Who guards my son with old fidelity,
Shall bring him hither from his tower by night
Lockt in a sleep so fast as by my art
I rivet to within a link of death,
But yet from death so far, that next day's dawn
Shall wake him up upon the royal bed,
Complete in consciousness and faculty,
When with all princely pomp and retinue
My loyal Peers with due obeisance
Shall hail him Segismund, the Prince of Poland.
Then if with any show of human kindness
He fling discredit, not upon the stars,
But upon me, their misinterpreter,
With all apology mistaken age
Can make to youth it never meant to harm,
To my son's forehead will I shift the crown
I long have wish'd upon a younger brow;
And in religious humiliation,
For what of worn-out age remains to me,
Entreat my pardon both of Heaven and him
For tempting destinies beyond my reach.
But if, as I misdoubt, at his first step
The hoof of the predicted savage shows;
Before predicted mischief can be done,
The self-same sleep that loosed him from the chain

Shall re-consign him, not to loose again.
Then shall I, having lost that heir direct,
Look solely to my sisters' children twain
Each of a claim so equal as divides
The voice of Poland to their several sides,
But, as I trust, to be entwined ere long
Into one single wreath so fair and strong
As shall at once all difference atone,
And cease the realm's division with their own.
Cousins and Princes, Peers and Councillors,
Such is the purport of this invitation,
And such is my design. Whose furtherance
If not as Sovereign, if not as Seer,
Yet one whom these white locks, if nothing else,
to patient acquiescence consecrate,
I now demand and even supplicate.

AST.
Such news, and from such lips, may well suspend
The tongue to loyal answer most attuned;
But if to me as spokesman of my faction
Your Highness looks for answer; I reply
For one and all—Let Segismund, whom now
We first hear tell of as your living heir,
Appear, and but in your sufficient eye
Approve himself worthy to be your son,
Then we will hail him Poland's rightful heir.
What says my cousin?

EST.
Ay, with all my heart.
But if my youth and sex upbraid me not

That I should dare ask of so wise a king—

KING.
Ask, ask, fair cousin! Nothing, I am sure,
Not well consider'd; nay, if 'twere, yet nothing
But pardonable from such lips as those.

EST.
Then, with your pardon, Sir—if Segismund,
My cousin, whom I shall rejoice to hail
As Prince of Poland too, as you propose,
Be to a trial coming upon which
More, as I think, than life itself depends,
Why, Sir, with sleep-disorder'd senses brought
To this uncertain contest with his stars?

KING.
Well ask'd indeed! As wisely be it answer'd!
Because it is uncertain, see you not?
For as I think I can discern between
The sudden flaws of a sleep-startled man,
And of the savage thing we have to dread;
If but bewilder'd, dazzled, and uncouth,
As might the sanest and the civilest
In circumstance so strange—nay, more than that,
If moved to any out-break short of blood,
All shall be well with him; and how much more,
If 'mid the magic turmoil of the change,
He shall so calm a resolution show
As scarce to reel beneath so great a blow!
But if with savage passion uncontroll'd
He lay about him like the brute foretold,

And must as suddenly be caged again;
Then what redoubled anguish and despair,
From that brief flash of blissful liberty
Remitted—and for ever—to his chain!
Which so much less, if on the stage of glory
Enter'd and exited through such a door
Of sleep as makes a dream of all between.

EST.
Oh kindly answer, Sir, to question that
To charitable courtesy less wise
Might call for pardon rather!
I shall now Gladly, what, uninstructed, loyally
I should have waited.

AST.
Your Highness doubts not me,
Nor how my heart follows my cousin's lips,
Whatever way the doubtful balance fall,
Still loyal to your bidding.

OMNES.
So say all.

KING.
I hoped, and did expect, of all no less—
And sure no sovereign ever needed more
From all who owe him love or loyalty.
For what a strait of time I stand upon,
When to this issue not alone I bring
My son your Prince, but e'en myself your King:
And, whichsoever way for him it turn,
Of less than little honour to myself.

For if this coming trial justify
My thus withholding from my son his right,
Is not the judge himself justified in
The father's shame? And if the judge proved wrong,
My son withholding from his right thus long,
Shame and remorse to judge and father both:
Unless remorse and shame together drown'd
In having what I flung for worthless found.
But come—already weary with your travel,
And ill refresh'd by this strange history,
Until the hours that draw the sun from heaven
Unite us at the customary board,
Each to his several chamber: you to rest;
I to contrive with old Clotaldo best
The method of a stranger thing than old
Time has a yet among his records told.

Exeunt.

ACT II

SCENE I—A Throne-room in the Palace. Music within.

(Enter King and Clotaldo, meeting a Lord in waiting)

KING.
You, for a moment beckon'd from your office,
Tell me thus far how goes it. In due time
The potion left him?

LORD.
At the very hour
To which your Highness temper'd it.
Yet not So wholly but some lingering mist still hung
About his dawning senses—which to clear,
We fill'd and handed him a morning drink
With sleep's specific antidote suffused;
And while with princely raiment we invested
What nature surely modell'd for a Prince—
All but the sword—as you directed—

KING.
Ay—

LORD.
If not too loudly, yet emphatically

Still with the title of a Prince address'd him.

KING.
How bore he that?

LORD.
With all the rest, my liege,
I will not say so like one in a dream
As one himself misdoubting that he dream'd.

KING.
So far so well, Clotaldo, either way,
And best of all if tow'rd the worse I dread.
But yet no violence?

LORD.
At most, impatience;
Wearied perhaps with importunities
We yet were bound to offer.

KING.
Oh, Clotaldo!
Though thus far well, yet would myself had drunk
The potion he revives from! such suspense
Crowds all the pulses of life's residue
Into the present moment; and, I think,
Whichever way the trembling scale may turn,
Will leave the crown of Poland for some one
To wait no longer than the setting sun!

CLO.
Courage, my liege! The curtain is undrawn,
And each must play his part out manfully,

Leaving the rest to heaven.

KING.

Whose written words
If I should misinterpret or transgress!
But as you say—
(To the Lord, who exit.)
You, back to him at once;
Clotaldo, you, when he is somewhat used
To the new world of which they call him Prince,
Where place and face, and all, is strange to him,
With your known features and familiar garb
Shall then, as chorus to the scene, accost him,
And by such earnest of that old and too
Familiar world, assure him of the new.
Last in the strange procession, I myself
Will by one full and last development
Complete the plot for that catastrophe
That he must put to all; God grant it be
The crown of Poland on his brows!—Hark! hark!—
Was that his voice within!—Now louder—Oh,
Clotaldo, what! so soon begun to roar!—
Again! above the music—But betide
What may, until the moment, we must hide.

(Exeunt King and Clotaldo.)

SEGISMUND (within).

Forbear! I stifle with your perfume! Cease
Your crazy salutations! peace, I say
Begone, or let me go, ere I go mad
With all this babble, mummery, and glare,
For I am growing dangerous—Air! room! air!—

(He rushes in. Music ceases.)
Oh but to save the reeling brain from wreck
With its bewilder'd senses!
(He covers his eyes for a while.)
What! E'en now
That Babel left behind me, but my eyes
Pursued by the same glamour, that—unless
Alike bewitch'd too—the confederate sense
Vouches for palpable: bright-shining floors
That ring hard answer back to the stamp'd heel,
And shoot up airy columns marble-cold,
That, as they climb, break into golden leaf
And capital, till they embrace aloft
In clustering flower and fruitage over walls
Hung with such purple curtain as the West
Fringes with such a gold; or over-laid
With sanguine-glowing semblances of men,
Each in his all but living action busied,
Or from the wall they look from, with fix'd eyes
Pursuing me; and one most strange of all
That, as I pass'd the crystal on the wall,
Look'd from it—left it—and as I return,
Returns, and looks me face to face again—
Unless some false reflection of my brain,
The outward semblance of myself—Myself?
How know that tawdry shadow for myself,
But that it moves as I move; lifts his hand
With mine; each motion echoing so close
The immediate suggestion of the will
In which myself I recognize—Myself!—
What, this fantastic Segismund the same
Who last night, as for all his nights before,
Lay down to sleep in wolf-skin on the ground

In a black turret which the wolf howl'd round,
And woke again upon a golden bed,
Round which as clouds about a rising sun,
In scarce less glittering caparison,
Gather'd gay shapes that, underneath a breeze
Of music, handed him upon their knees
The wine of heaven in a cup of gold,
And still in soft melodious under-song
Hailing me Prince of Poland!—'Segismund,'
They said, 'Our Prince! The Prince of Poland!' and
Again, 'Oh, welcome, welcome, to his own,
'Our own Prince Segismund—' Oh, but a blast—
One blast of the rough mountain air! one look
At the grim features—
(He goes to the window.)
What they disvizor'd also! shatter'd chaos
Cast into stately shape and masonry,
Between whose channel'd and perspective sides
Compact with rooted towers, and flourishing
To heaven with gilded pinnacle and spire,
Flows the live current ever to and fro
With open aspect and free step!—
Clotaldo! Clotaldo!—calling as one scarce dares call
For him who suddenly might break the spell
One fears to walk without him—
Why, that I, With unencumber'd step as any there,
Go stumbling through my glory—feeling for
That iron leading-string—ay, for myself—
For that fast-anchor'd self of yesterday,
Of yesterday, and all my life before,
Ere drifted clean from self-identity
Upon the fluctuation of to-day's
Mad whirling circumstance!—

And, fool, why not? If reason, sense, and self-identity
Obliterated from a worn-out brain,
Art thou not maddest striving to be sane,
And catching at that Self of yesterday
That, like a leper's rags, best flung away!
Or if not mad, then dreaming—dreaming?—well—
Dreaming then—Or, if self to self be true,
Not mock'd by that, but as poor souls have been
By those who wrong'd them, to give wrong new relish?
Or have those stars indeed they told me of
As masters of my wretched life of old,
Into some happier constellation roll'd,
And brought my better fortune out on earth
Clear as themselves in heaven!—Prince Segismund
They call'd me—and at will I shook them off—
Will they return again at my command
Again to call me so?—Within there!
You! Segismund calls—Prince Segismund—

(He has seated himself on the throne.
Enter Chamberlain, with lords in waiting.)

CHAMB.
I rejoice
That unadvised of any but the voice
Of royal instinct in the blood, your Highness
Has ta'en the chair that you were born to fill.

SEG.
The chair?

CHAMB.
The royal throne of Poland, Sir,

Which may your Royal Highness keep as long
As he that now rules from it shall have ruled
When heaven has call'd him to itself.

SEG.
When he?—

CHAMB.
Your royal father, King Basilio, Sir.

SEG.
My royal father—King Basilio.
You see I answer but as Echo does,
Not knowing what she listens or repeats.
This is my throne—this is my palace—Oh,
But this out of the window?—

CHAMB.
Warsaw, Sir, Your capital—

SEG.
And all the moving people?

CHAMB.
Your subjects and your vassals like ourselves.

SEG.
Ay, ay—my subjects—in my capital—
Warsaw—and I am Prince of it—You see
It needs much iteration to strike sense
Into the human echo.

CHAMB.
Left awhile
In the quick brain, the word will quickly to
Full meaning blow.

SEG.
You think so?

CHAMB.
And meanwhile
Lest our obsequiousness, which means no worse
Than customary honour to the Prince
We most rejoice to welcome, trouble you,
Should we retire again? or stand apart?
Or would your Highness have the music play
Again, which meditation, as they say,
So often loves to float upon?

SEG.
The music?
No—yes—perhaps the trumpet—
(Aside)
Yet if that
Brought back the troop!

A LORD.
The trumpet! There again
How trumpet-like spoke out the blood of Poland!

CHAMB.
Before the morning is far up, your Highness
Will have the trumpet marshalling your soldiers

Under the Palace windows.

SEG.
Ah, my soldiers—
My soldiers—not black-vizor'd?—

CHAMB.
Sir?

SEG.
No matter.
But—one thing—for a moment—in your ear—
Do you know one Clotaldo?

CHAMB.
Oh, my Lord,
He and myself together, I may say,
Although in different vocations,
Have silver'd in your royal father's service;
And, as I trust, with both of us a few
White hairs to fall in yours.

SEG.
Well said, well said!
Basilio, my father—well—Clotaldo
Is he my kinsman too?

CHAMB.
Oh, my good Lord,
A General simply in your Highness' service,
Than whom your Highness has no trustier.

SEG.
Ay, so you said before, I think. And you
With that white wand of yours—
Why, now I think on't, I have read of such
A silver-hair'd magician with a wand,
Who in a moment, with a wave of it,
Turn'd rags to jewels, clowns to emperors,
By some benigner magic than the stars
Spirited poor good people out of hand
From all their woes; in some enchanted sleep
Carried them off on cloud or dragon-back
Over the mountains, over the wide Deep,
And set them down to wake in Fairyland.

CHAMB.
Oh, my good Lord, you laugh at me—and I
Right glad to make you laugh at such a price:
You know me no enchanter: if I were,
I and my wand as much as your Highness',
As now your chamberlain—

SEG.
My chamberlain?—
And these that follow you?—

CHAMB.
On you, my Lord,
Your Highness' lords in waiting.

SEG.
Lords in waiting.
Well, I have now learn'd to repeat, I think,

If only but by rote—This is my palace,
And this my throne—which unadvised—
And that Out of the window there my Capital;
And all the people moving up and down
My subjects and my vassals like yourselves,
My chamberlain—and lords in waiting—and
Clotaldo—and Clotaldo?—
You are an aged, and seem a reverend man—
You do not—though his fellow-officer—
You do not mean to mock me?

CHAMB.
Oh, my Lord!

SEG.
Well then—If no magician, as you say,
Yet setting me a riddle, that my brain,
With all its senses whirling, cannot solve,
Yourself or one of these with you must answer—
How I—that only last night fell asleep
Not knowing that the very soil of earth
I lay down—chain'd—to sleep upon was Poland—
Awake to find myself the Lord of it,
With Lords, and Generals, and Chamberlains,
And ev'n my very Gaoler, for my vassals!
Enter suddenly Clotaldo

CLOTALDO.
Stand all aside
That I may put into his hand the clue
To lead him out of this amazement. Sir,
Vouchsafe your Highness from my bended knee

Receive my homage first.

SEG.
Clotaldo! What,
At last—his old self—undisguised where all
Is masquerade—to end it!—You kneeling too!
What! have the stars you told me long ago
Laid that old work upon you, added this,
That, having chain'd your prisoner so long,
You loose his body now to slay his wits,
Dragging him—how I know not—whither scarce
I understand—dressing him up in all
This frippery, with your dumb familiars
Disvizor'd, and their lips unlock'd to lie,
Calling him Prince and King, and, madman-like,
Setting a crown of straw upon his head?

CLO.
Would but your Highness, as indeed I now
Must call you—and upon his bended knee
Never bent Subject more devotedly—
However all about you, and perhaps
You to yourself incomprehensiblest,
But rest in the assurance of your own
Sane waking senses, by these witnesses
Attested, till the story of it all,
Of which I bring a chapter, be reveal'd,
Assured of all you see and hear as neither
Madness nor mockery—

SEG.
What then? CLO.

All it seems:
This palace with its royal garniture;
This capital of which it is the eye,
With all its temples, marts, and arsenals;
This realm of which this city is the head,
With all its cities, villages, and tilth,
Its armies, fleets, and commerce; all your own;
And all the living souls that make them up,
From those who now, and those who shall, salute you,
Down to the poorest peasant of the realm,
Your subjects—Who, though now their mighty voice
Sleeps in the general body unapprized,
Wait but a word from those about you now
To hail you Prince of Poland, Segismund.

SEG.
All this is so?

CLO.
As sure as anything
Is, or can be.

SEG.
You swear it on the faith
You taught me—elsewhere?—

CLO (kissing the hilt of his sword).
Swear it upon this Symbol,
and champion of the holy faith
I wear it to defend.

SEG (to himself).
My eyes have not deceived me, nor my ears,

With this transfiguration, nor the strain
Of royal welcome that arose and blew,
Breathed from no lying lips, along with it.
For here Clotaldo comes, his own old self,
Who, if not Lie and phantom with the rest—
(Aloud)
Well, then, all this is thus.
For have not these fine people told me so,
And you, Clotaldo, sworn it? And the Why
And Wherefore are to follow by and bye!
And yet—and yet—why wait for that which you
Who take your oath on it can answer—and
Indeed it presses hard upon my brain—
What I was asking of these gentlemen
When you came in upon us; how it is
That I—the Segismund you know so long
No longer than the sun that rose to-day
Rose—and from what you know—
Rose to be Prince of Poland?

CLO.
So to be
Acknowledged and entreated, Sir.

SEG.
So be
Acknowledged and entreated—
Well—But if now by all, by some at least
So known—if not entreated—heretofore—
Though not by you—For, now I think again,
Of what should be your attestation worth,
You that of all my questionable subjects
Who knowing what, yet left me where I was,

You least of all, Clotaldo, till the dawn
Of this first day that told it to myself?

CLO.
Oh, let your Highness draw the line across
Fore-written sorrow, and in this new dawn
Bury that long sad night.

SEG.
Not ev'n the Dead,
Call'd to the resurrection of the blest,
Shall so directly drop all memory
Of woes and wrongs foregone!

CLO.
But not resent—
Purged by the trial of that sorrow past
For full fruition of their present bliss.

SEG.
But leaving with the Judge what, till this earth
Be cancell'd in the burning heavens, He leaves
His earthly delegates to execute,
Of retribution in reward to them
And woe to those who wrong'd them—
Not as you, Not you, Clotaldo, knowing not—And yet
Ev'n to the guiltiest wretch in all the realm,
Of any treason guilty short of that,
Stern usage—but assuredly not knowing,
Not knowing 'twas your sovereign lord, Clotaldo,
You used so sternly.

CLO.
Ay, sir; with the same
Devotion and fidelity that now
Does homage to him for my sovereign.

SEG.
Fidelity that held his Prince in chains!

CLO.
Fidelity more fast than had it loosed him—

SEG.
Ev'n from the very dawn of consciousness
Down at the bottom of the barren rocks,
Where scarce a ray of sunshine found him out,
In which the poorest beggar of my realm
At least to human-full proportion grows—
Me! Me—whose station was the kingdom's top
To flourish in, reaching my head to heaven,
And with my branches overshadowing
The meaner growth below!

CLO.
Still with the same Fidelity—

SEG.
To me!—

CLO.
Ay, sir, to you,
Through that divine allegiance upon which
All Order and Authority is based;

Which to revolt against—

SEG.
Were to revolt
Against the stars, belike!

CLO.
And him who reads them;
And by that right, and by the sovereignty
He wears as you shall wear it after him;
Ay, one to whom yourself—
Yourself, ev'n more than any subject here,
Are bound by yet another and more strong
Allegiance—King Basilio—your Father—

SEG.
Basilio—King—my father!—

CLO.
Oh, my Lord,
Let me beseech you on my bended knee,
For your own sake—for Poland's—and for his,
Who, looking up for counsel to the skies,
Did what he did under authority
To which the kings of earth themselves are subject,
And whose behest not only he that suffers,
But he that executes, not comprehends,
But only He that orders it—

SEG.
The King—
My father!—Either I am mad already,
Or that way driving fast—or I should know

That fathers do not use their children so,
Or men were loosed from all allegiance
To fathers, kings, and heaven that order'd all.
But, mad or not, my hour is come, and I
Will have my reckoning—Either you lie,
Under the skirt of sinless majesty
Shrouding your treason; or if that indeed,
Guilty itself, take refuge in the stars
That cannot hear the charge, or disavow—
You, whether doer or deviser, who
Come first to hand, shall pay the penalty
By the same hand you owe it to—
(Seizing Clotaldo's sword and about to strike him.)
(Enter Rosaura suddenly.)
ROSAURA.
Fie, my Lord—forbear,
What! a young hand raised against silver hair!—
(She retreats through the crowd.)

SEG.
Stay! stay! What come and vanish'd as before—
I scarce remember how—but—

(Voices within. Room for Astolfo,
Duke of Muscovy!) (Enter Astolfo)

ASTOLFO.
Welcome, thrice welcome, the auspicious day,
When from the mountain where he darkling lay,
The Polish sun into the firmament
Sprung all the brighter for his late ascent,
And in meridian glory—

SEG.
Where is he?
Why must I ask this twice?—

A LORD.
The Page, my Lord?
I wonder at his boldness—

SEG.
But I tell you
He came with Angel written in his face
As now it is, when all was black as hell
About, and none of you who now—he came,
And Angel-like flung me a shining sword
To cut my way through darkness; and again
Angel-like wrests it from me in behalf
Of one—whom I will spare for sparing him:
But he must come and plead with that same voice
That pray'd for me—in vain.

CHAMB.
He is gone for,
And shall attend your pleasure, sir. Meanwhile,
Will not your Highness, as in courtesy,
Return your royal cousin's greeting?

SEG.
Whose?

CHAMB.
Astolfo, Duke of Muscovy, my Lord,
Saluted, and with gallant compliment

Welcomed you to your royal title.

SEG. (to Astolfo). Oh—
You knew of this then?

AST.
Knew of what, my Lord?

SEG.
That I was Prince of Poland all the while,
And you my subject?

AST.
Pardon me, my Lord,
But some few hours ago myself I learn'd
Your dignity; but, knowing it, no more
Than when I knew it not, your subject.

SEG.
What then?

AST.
Your Highness' chamberlain ev'n now has told you;
Astolfo, Duke of Muscovy,
Your father's sister's son; your cousin, sir:
And who as such, and in his own right Prince,
Expects from you the courtesy he shows.

CHAMB.
His Highness is as yet unused to Court,
And to the ceremonious interchange
Of compliment, especially to those

Who draw their blood from the same royal fountain.

SEG.
Where is the lad? I weary of all this—
Prince, cousins, chamberlains, and compliments—
Where are my soldiers? Blow the trumpet, and
With one sharp blast scatter these butterflies
And bring the men of iron to my side,
With whom a king feels like a king indeed!

(Voices within. Within there! room for the
Princess Estrella!)
(Enter Estrella with Ladies.)

ESTRELLA.
Welcome, my Lord, right welcome to the throne
That much too long has waited for your coming:
And, in the general voice of Poland, hear
A kinswoman and cousin's no less sincere.

SEG.
Ay, this is welcome-worth indeed,
And cousin cousin-worth! Oh, I have thus
Over the threshold of the mountain seen,
Leading a bevy of fair stars, the moon
Enter the court of heaven—My kinswoman!
My cousin! But my subject?—

EST.
If you please
To count your cousin for your subject, sir,
You shall not find her a disloyal.

SEG.
Oh,
But there are twin stars in that heavenly face,
That now I know for having over-ruled
Those evil ones that darken'd all my past
And brought me forth from that captivity
To be the slave of her who set me free.

EST.
Indeed, my Lord, these eyes have no such power
Over the past or present: but perhaps
They brighten at your welcome to supply
The little that a lady's speech commends;
And in the hope that, let whichever be
The other's subject, we may both be friends.

SEG.
Your hand to that—But why does this warm hand
Shoot a cold shudder through me?

EST.
In revenge
For likening me to that cold moon, perhaps.

SEG.
Oh, but the lip whose music tells me so
Breathes of a warmer planet, and that lip
Shall remedy the treason of the hand!
(He catches to embrace her.)

EST.
Release me, sir!

CHAMB.
And pardon me, my Lord.
This lady is a Princess absolute,
As Prince he is who just saluted you,
And claims her by affiance.

SEG.
Hence, old fool,
For ever thrusting that white stick of yours
Between me and my pleasure!

AST.
This cause is mine. Forbear, sir—

SEG.
What, sir mouth-piece, you again?

AST.
My Lord, I waive your insult to myself
In recognition of the dignity
You yet are new to, and that greater still
You look in time to wear. But for this lady—
Whom, if my cousin now, I hope to claim
Henceforth by yet a nearer, dearer name—

SEG.
And what care I? She is my cousin too:
And if you be a Prince—well, am not I
Lord of the very soil you stand upon?
By that, and by that right beside of blood
That like a fiery fountain hitherto
Pent in the rock leaps toward her at her touch,
Mine, before all the cousins in Muscovy!

You call me Prince of Poland, and yourselves
My subjects—traitors therefore to this hour,
Who let me perish all my youth away
Chain'd there among the mountains; till, forsooth,
Terrified at your treachery foregone,
You spirit me up here, I know not how,
Popinjay-like invest me like yourselves,
Choke me with scent and music that I loathe,
And, worse than all the music and the scent,
With false, long-winded, fulsome compliment,
That 'Oh, you are my subjects!' and in word
Reiterating still obedience,
Thwart me in deed at every step I take:
When just about to wreak a just revenge
Upon that old arch-traitor of you all,
Filch from my vengeance him I hate; and him
I loved—the first and only face—till this—
I cared to look on in your ugly court—
And now when palpably I grasp at last
What hitherto but shadow'd in my dreams—
Affiances and interferences,
The first who dares to meddle with me more—
Princes and chamberlains and counsellors,
Touch her who dares!—

AST.
That dare I—

SEG. (seizing him by the throat).
You dare!

CHAMB.
My Lord!—

A LORD.
His strength's a lion's—
(Voices within. The King! The King!—)
(Enter King.)

A LORD.
And on a sudden how he stands at gaze
As might a wolf just fasten'd on his prey,
Glaring at a suddenly encounter'd lion.

KING.
And I that hither flew with open arms
To fold them round my son, must now return
To press them to an empty heart again!
(He sits on the throne.)

SEG.
That is the King?—My father?
(After a long pause.)
I have heard
That sometimes some blind instinct has been known
To draw to mutual recognition those
Of the same blood, beyond all memory
Divided, or ev'n never met before.
I know not how this is—perhaps in brutes
That live by kindlier instincts—but I know
That looking now upon that head whose crown
Pronounces him a sovereign king, I feel
No setting of the current in my blood
Tow'rd him as sire. How is't with you, old man,
Tow'rd him they call your son?—

KING.
Alas! Alas!

SEG.
Your sorrow, then?

KING.
Beholding what I do.

SEG.
Ay, but how know this sorrow that has grown
And moulded to this present shape of man,
As of your own creation?

KING.
Ev'n from birth.

SEG.
But from that hour to this, near, as I think,
Some twenty such renewals of the year
As trace themselves upon the barren rocks,
I never saw you, nor you me—unless,
Unless, indeed, through one of those dark masks
Through which a son might fail to recognize
The best of fathers.

KING.
Be that as you will:
But, now we see each other face to face,
Know me as you I know; which did I not,
By whatsoever signs, assuredly
You were not here to prove it at my risk.

SEG.
You are my father.
And is it true then, as Clotaldo swears,
'Twas you that from the dawning birth of one
Yourself brought into being,—you, I say,
Who stole his very birthright; not alone
That secondary and peculiar right
Of sovereignty, but even that prime
Inheritance that all men share alike,
And chain'd him—chain'd him!—like a wild beast's whelp.
Among as savage mountains, to this hour?
Answer if this be thus.

KING.
Oh, Segismund,
In all that I have done that seems to you,
And, without further hearing, fairly seems,
Unnatural and cruel—'twas not I,
But One who writes His order in the sky
I dared not misinterpret nor neglect,
Who knows with what reluctance—

SEG.
Oh, those stars,
Those stars, that too far up from human blame
To clear themselves, or careless of the charge,
Still bear upon their shining shoulders all
The guilt men shift upon them!

KING.
Nay, but think:
Not only on the common score of kind,
But that peculiar count of sovereignty—

If not behind the beast in brain as heart,
How should I thus deal with my innocent child,
Doubly desired, and doubly dear when come,
As that sweet second-self that all desire,
And princes more than all, to root themselves
By that succession in their people's hearts,
Unless at that superior Will, to which
Not kings alone, but sovereign nature bows?

SEG.
And what had those same stars to tell of me
That should compel a father and a king
So much against that double instinct?

KING.
That,
Which I have brought you hither, at my peril,
Against their written warning, to disprove,
By justice, mercy, human kindliness.

SEG.
And therefore made yourself their instrument
To make your son the savage and the brute
They only prophesied?—
Are you not afear'd,
Lest, irrespective as such creatures are
Of such relationship, the brute you made
Revenge the man you marr'd—like sire, like son.
To do by you as you by me have done?

KING.
You never had a savage heart from me;

I may appeal to Poland.

SEG.
Then from whom?
If pure in fountain, poison'd by yourself
When scarce begun to flow.—
To make a man Not, as I see, degraded from the mould
I came from, nor compared to those about,
And then to throw your own flesh to the dogs!—
Why not at once, I say, if terrified
At the prophetic omens of my birth,
Have drown'd or stifled me, as they do whelps
Too costly or too dangerous to keep?

KING.
That, living, you might learn to live, and rule
Yourself and Poland.

SEG.
By the means you took
To spoil for either?

KING.
Nay, but, Segismund!
You know not—cannot know—happily wanting
The sad experience on which knowledge grows,
How the too early consciousness of power
Spoils the best blood; nor whether for your long
Constrain'd disheritance (which, but for me,
Remember, and for my relenting love
Bursting the bond of fate, had been eternal)
You have not now a full indemnity;
Wearing the blossom of your youth unspent

In the voluptuous sunshine of a court,
That often, by too early blossoming,
Too soon deflowers the rose of royalty.

SEG.
Ay, but what some precocious warmth may spill,
May not an early frost as surely kill?

KING.
But, Segismund, my son, whose quick discourse
Proves I have not extinguish'd and destroy'd
The Man you charge me with extinguishing,
However it condemn me for the fault
Of keeping a good light so long eclipsed, Reflect!
This is the moment upon which
Those stars, whose eyes, although we see them not,
By day as well as night are on us still,
Hang watching up in the meridian heaven
Which way the balance turns; and if to you—
As by your dealing God decide it may,
To my confusion!—let me answer it
Unto yourself alone, who shall at once
Approve yourself to be your father's judge,
And sovereign of Poland in his stead,
By justice, mercy, self-sobriety,
And all the reasonable attributes
Without which, impotent to rule himself,
Others one cannot, and one must not rule;
But which if you but show the blossom of—
All that is past we shall but look upon
As the first out-fling of a generous nature
Rioting in first liberty; and if
This blossom do but promise such a flower

As promises in turn its kindly fruit:
Forthwith upon your brows the royal crown,
That now weighs heavy on my aged brows,
I will devolve; and while I pass away
Into some cloister, with my Maker there
To make my peace in penitence and prayer,
Happily settle the disorder'd realm
That now cries loudly for a lineal heir.

SEG.
And so—
When the crown falters on your shaking head,
And slips the sceptre from your palsied hand,
And Poland for her rightful heir cries out;
When not only your stol'n monopoly
Fails you of earthly power, but 'cross the grave
The judgment-trumpet of another world
Calls you to count for your abuse of this;
Then, oh then, terrified by the double danger,
You drag me from my den—
Boast not of giving up at last the power
You can no longer hold, and never rightly
Held, but in fee for him you robb'd it from;
And be assured your Savage, once let loose,
Will not be caged again so quickly; not
By threat or adulation to be tamed,
Till he have had his quarrel out with those
Who made him what he is.

KING.
Beware! Beware!
Subdue the kindled Tiger in your eye,

Nor dream that it was sheer necessity
Made me thus far relax the bond of fate,
And, with far more of terror than of hope
Threaten myself, my people, and the State.
Know that, if old, I yet have vigour left
To wield the sword as well as wear the crown;
And if my more immediate issue fail,
Not wanting scions of collateral blood,
Whose wholesome growth shall more than compensate
For all the loss of a distorted stem.

SEG.
That will I straightway bring to trial—Oh,
After a revelation such as this,
The Last Day shall have little left to show
Of righted wrong and villainy requited!
Nay, Judgment now beginning upon earth,
Myself, methinks, in sight of all my wrongs,
Appointed heaven's avenging minister,
Accuser, judge, and executioner
Sword in hand, cite the guilty—First, as worst,
The usurper of his son's inheritance;
Him and his old accomplice, time and crime
Inveterate, and unable to repay
The golden years of life they stole away.
What, does he yet maintain his state, and keep
The throne he should be judged from?
Down with him,
That I may trample on the false white head
So long has worn my crown!
Where are my soldiers?
Of all my subjects and my vassals here

Not one to do my bidding? Hark! A trumpet!
The trumpet—

(He pauses as the trumpet sounds as in Act I.,
and masked Soldiers gradually fill in behind the Throne.)

KING (rising before his throne).
Ay, indeed, the trumpet blows
A memorable note, to summon those
Who, if forthwith you fall not at the feet
Of him whose head you threaten with the dust,
Forthwith shall draw the curtain of the Past
About you; and this momentary gleam
Of glory that you think to hold life-fast,
So coming, so shall vanish, as a dream.

SEG.
He prophesies; the old man prophesies;
And, at his trumpet's summons, from the tower
The leash-bound shadows loosen'd after me
My rising glory reach and over-lour—
But, reach not I my height, he shall not hold,
But with me back to his own darkness!
(He dashes toward the throne and is enclosed by the soldiers.)
Traitors!
Hold off! Unhand me!—
Am not I your king?
And you would strangle him!—
But I am breaking with an inward Fire
Shall scorch you off, and wrap me on the wings
Of conflagration from a kindled pyre
Of lying prophecies and prophet-kings

Above the extinguish'd stars—Reach me the sword
He flung me—Fill me such a bowl of wine
As that you woke the day with—

KING.
And shall close,—
But of the vintage that Clotaldo knows.

(Exeunt.)

ACT III

SCENE I.—The Tower, etc., as in Act I. Scene I.

(Segismund, as at first, and Clotaldo.)

CLOTALDO.
Princes and princesses, and counsellors
Fluster'd to right and left—my life made at—
But that was nothing
Even the white-hair'd, venerable
King Seized on—Indeed, you made wild work of it;
And so discover'd in your outward action,
Flinging your arms about you in your sleep,
Grinding your teeth—and, as I now remember,
Woke mouthing out judgment and execution,
On those about you.

SEG.
Ay, I did indeed.

CLO.
Ev'n now your eyes stare wild; your hair stands up—
Your pulses throb and flutter, reeling still
Under the storm of such a dream—

SEG.
A dream!
That seem'd as swearable reality
As what I wake in now.

CLO.
Ay—wondrous how
Imagination in a sleeping brain
Out of the uncontingent senses draws
Sensations strong as from the real touch;
That we not only laugh aloud, and drench
With tears our pillow; but in the agony
Of some imaginary conflict, fight
And struggle—ev'n as you did; some, 'tis thought,
Under the dreamt-of stroke of death have died.

SEG.
And what so very strange too—In that world
Where place as well as people all was strange, Ev'n
I almost as strange unto myself,
You only, you, Clotaldo—you, as much
And palpably yourself as now you are,
Came in this very garb you ever wore,
By such a token of the past, you said,
To assure me of that seeming present.

CLO.
Ay?

SEG.
Ay; and even told me of the very stars
You tell me here of—how in spite of them,

I was enlarged to all that glory.

CLO.
Ay, By the false spirits' nice contrivance thus
A little truth oft leavens all the false,
The better to delude us.

SEG.
For you know
'Tis nothing but a dream?

CLO.
Nay, you yourself
Know best how lately you awoke from that
You know you went to sleep on?—
Why, have you never dreamt the like before?

SEG.
Never, to such reality.

CLO.
Such dreams
Are oftentimes the sleeping exhalations
Of that ambition that lies smouldering
Under the ashes of the lowest fortune;
By which, when reason slumbers, or has lost
The reins of sensible comparison,
We fly at something higher than we are—
Scarce ever dive to lower—to be kings,
Or conquerors, crown'd with laurel or with gold,
Nay, mounting heaven itself on eagle wings.
Which, by the way, now that I think of it,
May furnish us the key to this high flight

That royal Eagle we were watching, and
Talking of as you went to sleep last night.

SEG.
Last night? Last night?

CLO.
Ay, do you not remember
Envying his immunity of flight,
As, rising from his throne of rock, he sail'd
Above the mountains far into the West,
That burn'd about him, while with poising wings
He darkled in it as a burning brand
Is seen to smoulder in the fire it feeds?

SEG.
Last night—last night—Oh, what a day was that
Between that last night and this sad To-day!

CLO.
And yet, perhaps,
Only some few dark moments, into which
Imagination, once lit up within
And unconditional of time and space,
Can pour infinities.

SEG.
And I remember
How the old man they call'd the King, who wore
The crown of gold about his silver hair,
And a mysterious girdle round his waist,
Just when my rage was roaring at its height,
And after which it all was dark again,

Bid me beware lest all should be a dream.

CLO.
Ay—there another specialty of dreams,
That once the dreamer 'gins to dream he dreams,
His foot is on the very verge of waking.

SEG.
Would it had been upon the verge of death
That knows no waking—
Lifting me up to glory, to fall back,
Stunn'd, crippled—wretcheder than ev'n before.

CLO.
Yet not so glorious, Segismund, if you
Your visionary honour wore so ill
As to work murder and revenge on those
Who meant you well.

SEG.
Who meant me!—me! their Prince
Chain'd like a felon—

CLO.
Stay, stay—Not so fast,
You dream'd the Prince, remember.

SEG.
Then in dream Revenged it only.

CLO.
True. But as they say

Dreams are rough copies of the waking soul
Yet uncorrected of the higher Will,
So that men sometimes in their dreams confess
An unsuspected, or forgotten, self;
One must beware to check—ay, if one may,
Stifle ere born, such passion in ourselves
As makes, we see, such havoc with our sleep,
And ill reacts upon the waking day.
And, by the bye, for one test, Segismund,
Between such swearable realities—
Since Dreaming, Madness, Passion, are akin
In missing each that salutary rein
Of reason, and the guiding will of man:
One test, I think, of waking sanity
Shall be that conscious power of self-control,
To curb all passion, but much most of all
That evil and vindictive, that ill squares
With human, and with holy canon less,
Which bids us pardon ev'n our enemies,
And much more those who, out of no ill will,
Mistakenly have taken up the rod
Which heaven, they think, has put into their hands.

SEG.
I think I soon shall have to try again—
Sleep has not yet done with me.

CLO.
Such a sleep.
Take my advice—'tis early yet—the sun
Scarce up above the mountain; go within,
And if the night deceived you, try anew

With morning; morning dreams they say come true.

SEG.
Oh, rather pray for me a sleep so fast
As shall obliterate dream and waking too.
(Exit into the tower.)

CLO.
So sleep; sleep fast: and sleep away those two
Night-potions, and the waking dream between
Which dream thou must believe; and, if to see
Again, poor Segismund! that dream must be.—
And yet, and yet, in these our ghostly lives,
Half night, half day, half sleeping, half awake,
How if our waking life, like that of sleep,
Be all a dream in that eternal life
To which we wake not till we sleep in death?
How if, I say, the senses we now trust
For date of sensible comparison,—
Ay, ev'n the Reason's self that dates with them,
Should be in essence or intensity
Hereafter so transcended, and awake
To a perceptive subtlety so keen
As to confess themselves befool'd before,
In all that now they will avouch for most?
One man—like this—but only so much longer
As life is longer than a summer's day,
Believed himself a king upon his throne,
And play'd at hazard with his fellows' lives,
Who cheaply dream'd away their lives to him.
The sailor dream'd of tossing on the flood:
The soldier of his laurels grown in blood:
The lover of the beauty that he knew

Must yet dissolve to dusty residue:
The merchant and the miser of his bags
Of finger'd gold; the beggar of his rags:
And all this stage of earth on which we seem
Such busy actors, and the parts we play'd,
Substantial as the shadow of a shade,
And Dreaming but a dream within a dream!

FIFE.
Was it not said, sir,
By some philosopher as yet unborn,
That any chimney-sweep who for twelve hours
Dreams himself king is happy as the king
Who dreams himself twelve hours a chimney-sweep?

CLO.
A theme indeed for wiser heads than yours
To moralize upon—How came you here?—

FIFE.
Not of my own will, I assure you, sir.
No matter for myself: but I would know
About my mistress—I mean, master—

CLO.
Oh, Now I remember—Well, your master-mistress
Is well, and deftly on its errand speeds,
As you shall—if you can but hold your tongue.
Can you?

FIFE.
I'd rather be at home again.

CLO.
Where you shall be the quicker if while here
You can keep silence.

FIFE.
I may whistle, then?
Which by the virtue of my name I do,
And also as a reasonable test
Of waking sanity—
CLO.
Well, whistle then;
And for another reason you forgot,
That while you whistle, you can chatter not.
Only remember—if you quit this pass—

FIFE.
(His rhymes are out, or he had call'd it spot)—

CLO.
A bullet brings you to.
I must forthwith to court to tell the King
The issue of this lamentable day,
That buries all his hope in night.
(To FIFE.)
Farewell. Remember.

FIFE.
But a moment—but a word!
When shall I see my mis—mas—

CLO.
Be content:
All in good time; and then, and not before,

Never to miss your master any more.
(Exit.)

FIFE.
Such talk of dreaming—dreaming—I begin
To doubt if I be dreaming I am Fife,
Who with a lad who call'd herself a boy
Because—I doubt there's some confusion here—
He wore no petticoat, came on a time
Riding from Muscovy on half a horse,
Who must have dreamt she was a horse entire,
To cant me off upon my hinder face
Under this tower, wall-eyed and musket-tongued,
With sentinels a-pacing up and down,
Crying All's well when all is far from well,
All the day long, and all the night, until
I dream—if what is dreaming be not waking—
Of bells a-tolling and processions rolling
With candles, crosses, banners, San-benitos,
Of which I wear the flamy-finingest,
Through streets and places throng'd with fiery faces
To some back platform—
Oh, I shall take a fire into my hand
With thinking of my own dear Muscovy—
Only just over that Sierra there,
By which we tumbled headlong into—
No-land. Now, if without a bullet after me,
I could but get a peep of my old home
Perhaps of my own mule to take me there—
All's still—perhaps the gentlemen within
Are dreaming it is night behind their masks—
God send 'em a good nightmare!—
Now then—Hark!

Voices—and up the rocks—and armed men
Climbing like cats—
Puss in the corner then.

(He hides.)
(Enter Soldiers cautiously up the rocks.)

CAPTAIN.
This is the frontier pass, at any rate,
Where Poland ends and Muscovy begins.

SOLDIER.
We must be close upon the tower, I know,
That half way up the mountain lies ensconced.

CAPT.
How know you that?

SOL.
He told me so—the Page
Who put us on the scent.

SOL. 2.
And, as I think,
Will soon be here to run it down with us.

CAPT.
Meantime, our horses on these ugly rocks
Useless, and worse than useless with their clatter—
Leave them behind, with one or two in charge,
And softly, softly, softly.

SOLDIERS.
—There it is!
—There what?
—The tower—the fortress—
—That the tower!—
—That mouse-trap!
We could pitch it down the rocks
With our own hands.
—The rocks it hangs among
Dwarf its proportions and conceal its strength;
Larger and stronger than you think.
—No matter;
No place for Poland's Prince to be shut up in.
At it at once!

CAPT.
No—no—I tell you wait—
Till those within give signal. For as yet
We know not who side with us, and the fort
Is strong in man and musket.

SOL.
Shame to wait
For odds with such a cause at stake.

CAPT.
Because
Of such a cause at stake we wait for odds—
For if not won at once, for ever lost:
For any long resistance on their part
Would bring Basilio's force to succour them
Ere we had rescued him we come to rescue.

So softly, softly, softly, still—

A SOLDIER (discovering Fife).
Hilloa!

SOLDIERS.
—Hilloa! Here's some one skulking—
—Seize and gag him!
—Stab him at once, say I: the only way
To make all sure.
—Hold, every man of you!
And down upon your knees!—
Why, 'tis the Prince!
—The Prince!—
—Oh, I should know him anywhere,
And anyhow disguised.
—But the Prince is chain'd.
—And of a loftier presence—
—'Tis he, I tell you;
Only bewilder'd as he was before.
God save your Royal Highness!
On our knees Beseech you answer us!

FIFE.
Just as you please.
Well—'tis this country's custom, I suppose,
To take a poor man every now and then
And set him ON the throne; just for the fun
Of tumbling him again into the dirt.
And now my turn is come. 'Tis very pretty.

SOL.
His wits have been distemper'd with their drugs.

But do you ask him, Captain.

CAPT.
On my knees,
And in the name of all who kneel with me,
I do beseech your Highness answer to
Your royal title.

FIFE.
Still, just as you please.
In my own poor opinion of myself—
But that may all be dreaming, which it seems
Is very much the fashion in this country
No Polish prince at all, but a poor lad
From Muscovy; where only help me back,
I promise never to contest the crown
Of Poland with whatever gentleman
You fancy to set up.

SOLDIERS.
—From Muscovy?
—A spy then—
—Of Astolfo's—
—Spy! a spy
—Hang him at once!

FIFE.
No, pray don't dream of that!

SOL.
How dared you then set yourself up for our
Prince Segismund?

FIFE.
I set up!—I like that
When 'twas yourselves be-siegesmunded me.

CAPT.
No matter—Look!—The signal from the tower.
Prince Segismund!

SOL. (from the tower).
Prince Segismund!

CAPT.
All's well. Clotaldo safe secured?—

SOL. (from the tower).
No—by ill luck,
Instead of coming in, as we had look'd for,
He sprang on horse at once, and off at gallop.

CAPT.
To Court, no doubt—a blunder that—
And yet Perchance a blunder that may work as well
As better forethought. Having no suspicion
So will he carry none where his not going
Were of itself suspicious. But of those
Within, who side with us?

SOL.
Oh, one and all
To the last man, persuaded or compell'd.

CAPT.
Enough: whatever be to be retrieved

No moment to be lost. For though
Clotaldo Have no revolt to tell of in the tower,
The capital will soon awake to ours,
And the King's force come blazing after us.
Where is the Prince?

SOL.
Within; so fast asleep
We woke him not ev'n striking off the chain
We had so cursedly help bind him with,
Not knowing what we did; but too ashamed
Not to undo ourselves what we had done.

CAPT.
No matter, nor by whosesoever hands,
Provided done. Come; we will bring him forth
Out of that stony darkness here abroad,
Where air and sunshine sooner shall disperse
The sleepy fume which they have drugg'd him with.

(They enter the tower, and thence bring out
Segismund asleep on a pallet, and set him in the middle of the stage.)

CAPT.
Still, still so dead asleep, the very noise
And motion that we make in carrying him
Stirs not a leaf in all the living tree.

SOLDIERS.
If living—But if by some inward blow
For ever and irrevocably fell'd
By what strikes deeper to the root than sleep?

—He's dead! He's dead! They've kill'd him—
—No—he breathes—
And the heart beats—and now he breathes again
Deeply, as one about to shake away
The load of sleep.

CAPT.
Come, let us all kneel round,
And with a blast of warlike instruments,
And acclamation of all loyal hearts,
Rouse and restore him to his royal right,
From which no royal wrong shall drive him more.
(They all kneel round his bed: trumpets, drums, etc.)

SOLDIERS.
—Segismund! Segismund! Prince Segismund!
—King Segismund! Down with Basilio!
—Down with Astolfo! Segismund our King! etc.
—He stares upon us wildly. He cannot speak.
—I said so—driv'n him mad.
—Speak to him, Captain.

CAPTAIN.
Oh Royal Segismund, our Prince and King,
Look on us—listen to us—answer us,
Your faithful soldiery and subjects, now
About you kneeling, but on fire to rise
And cleave a passage through your enemies,
Until we seat you on your lawful throne.
For though your father, King Basilio,
Now King of Poland, jealous of the stars
That prophesy his setting with your rise,
Here holds you ignominiously eclipsed,

And would Astolfo, Duke of Muscovy,
Mount to the throne of Poland after him;
So will not we, your loyal soldiery
And subjects; neither those of us now first
Apprised of your existence and your right:
Nor those that hitherto deluded by
Allegiance false, their vizors now fling down,
And craving pardon on their knees with us
For that unconscious disloyalty,
Offer with us the service of their blood;
Not only we and they; but at our heels
The heart, if not the bulk, of Poland follows
To join their voices and their arms with ours,
In vindicating with our lives our own
Prince Segismund to Poland and her throne.

SOLDIERS.
—Segismund, Segismund, Prince Segismund!
—Our own King Segismund, etc. (They all rise.)

SEG.
Again? So soon?—What, not yet done with me?
The sun is little higher up, I think,
Than when I last lay down,
To bury in the depth of your own sea
You that infest its shallows.

CAPT.
Sir!

SEG.
And now,
Not in a palace, not in the fine clothes

We all were in; but here, in the old place,
And in our old accoutrement—
Only your vizors off, and lips unlock'd
To mock me with that idle title—

CAPT.
Nay,
Indeed no idle title, but your own,
Then, now, and now for ever. For, behold,
Ev'n as I speak, the mountain passes fill
And bristle with the advancing soldiery
That glitters in your rising glory, sir;
And, at our signal, echo to our cry,
'Segismund, King of Poland!' etc.
(Shouts, trumpets, etc.)

SEG.
Oh, how cheap
The muster of a countless host of shadows,
As impotent to do with as to keep!
All this they said before—to softer music.

CAPT.
Soft music, sir, to what indeed were shadows,
That, following the sunshine of a Court,
Shall back be brought with it—if shadows still,
Yet to substantial reckoning.

SEG.
They shall?
The white-hair'd and white-wanded chamberlain,
So busy with his wand too—the old King
That I was somewhat hard on—he had been

Hard upon me—and the fine feather'd Prince
Who crow'd so loud—my cousin,—and another,
Another cousin, we will not bear hard on—
And—But Clotaldo?

CAPT.
Fled, my lord, but close Pursued; and then—

SEG.
Then, as he fled before,
And after he had sworn it on his knees,
Came back to take me—where I am!—
No more, No more of this! Away with you! Begone!
Whether but visions of ambitious night
That morning ought to scatter, or grown out
Of night's proportions you invade the day
To scare me from my little wits yet left,
Begone! I know I must be near awake,
Knowing I dream; or, if not at my voice,
Then vanish at the clapping of my hands,
Or take this foolish fellow for your sport:
Dressing me up in visionary glories,
Which the first air of waking consciousness
Scatters as fast as from the almander—
That, waking one fine morning in full flower,
One rougher insurrection of the breeze
Of all her sudden honour disadorns
To the last blossom, and she stands again
The winter-naked scare-crow that she was!

CAPT.
I know not what to do, nor what to say,
With all this dreaming; I begin to doubt

They have driv'n him mad indeed, and he and we
Are lost together.

A SOLDIER (to Captain).
Stay, stay; I remember—
Hark in your ear a moment.
(Whispers.)

CAPT.
So—so—so?—
Oh, now indeed I do not wonder, sir,
Your senses dazzle under practices
Which treason, shrinking from its own device,
Would now persuade you only was a dream;
But waking was as absolute as this
You wake in now, as some who saw you then,
Prince as you were and are, can testify:
Not only saw, but under false allegiance
Laid hands upon—

SOLDIER 1.
I, to my shame!

SOLDIER 2.
And I!

CAPT.
Who, to wipe out that shame, have been the first
To stir and lead us—Hark!
(Shouts, trumpets, etc.)

A SOLDIER.
Our forces, sir,

Challenging King Basilio's, now in sight,
And bearing down upon us.

CAPT.
Sir, you hear;
A little hesitation and delay,
And all is lost—your own right, and the lives
Of those who now maintain it at that cost;
With you all saved and won; without, all lost.
That former recognition of your right
Grant but a dream, if you will have it so;
Great things forecast themselves by shadows great:
Or will you have it, this like that dream too,
People, and place, and time itself, all dream
Yet, being in't, and as the shadows come
Quicker and thicker than you can escape,
Adopt your visionary soldiery,
Who, having struck a solid chain away,
Now put an airy sword into your hand,
And harnessing you piece-meal till you stand
Amidst us all complete in glittering,
If unsubstantial, steel—

ROSAURA (without).
The Prince! The Prince!

CAPT.
Who calls for him?

SOL.
The Page who spurr'd us hither,
And now, dismounted from a foaming horse—
(Enter Rosaura)

ROSAURA.
Where is—but where I need no further ask
Where the majestic presence, all in arms,
Mutely proclaims and vindicates himself.

FIFE.
My darling Lady-lord—

ROS.
My own good Fife,
Keep to my side—and silence!—
Oh, my Lord,
For the third time behold me here where first
You saw me, by a happy misadventure
Losing my own way here to find it out
For you to follow with these loyal men,
Adding the moment of my little cause
To yours; which, so much mightier as it is,
By a strange chance runs hand in hand with mine;
The self-same foe who now pretends your right,
Withholding mine—that, of itself alone,
I know the royal blood that runs in you
Would vindicate, regardless of your own:
The right of injured innocence; and, more,
Spite of this epicene attire, a woman's;
And of a noble stock I will not name
Till I, who brought it, have retrieved the shame.
Whom Duke Astolfo, Prince of Muscovy,
With all the solemn vows of wedlock won,
And would have wedded, as I do believe,
Had not the cry of Poland for a Prince
Call'd him from Muscovy to join the prize
Of Poland with the fair Estrella's eyes.

I, following him hither, as you saw,
Was cast upon these rocks; arrested by
Clotaldo: who, for an old debt of love
He owes my family, with all his might
Served, and had served me further, till my cause
Clash'd with his duty to his sovereign,
Which, as became a loyal subject, sir,
(And never sovereign had a loyaller,)
Was still his first. He carried me to Court,
Where, for the second time, I crossed your path;
Where, as I watch'd my opportunity,
Suddenly broke this public passion out;
Which, drowning private into public wrong,
Yet swiftlier sweeps it to revenge along.

SEG.
Oh God, if this be dreaming, charge it not
To burst the channel of enclosing sleep
And drown the waking reason! Not to dream
Only what dreamt shall once or twice again
Return to buzz about the sleeping brain
Till shaken off for ever—
But reassailing one so quick, so thick—
The very figure and the circumstance
Of sense-confess'd reality foregone
In so-call'd dream so palpably repeated,
The copy so like the original,
We know not which is which; and dream so-call'd
Itself inweaving so inextricably
Into the tissue of acknowledged truth;
The very figures that empeople it
Returning to assert themselves no phantoms
In something so much like meridian day,

And in the very place that not my worst
And veriest disenchanter shall deny
For the too well-remember'd theatre
Of my long tragedy—Strike up the drums!
If this be Truth, and all of us awake,
Indeed a famous quarrel is at stake:
If but a Vision I will see it out,
And, drive the Dream, I can but join the rout.

CAPT.
And in good time, sir, for a palpable
Touchstone of truth and rightful vengeance too,
Here is Clotaldo taken.

SOLDIERS.
In with him!
In with the traitor! (
Clotaldo brought in.)
SEG.
Ay, Clotaldo, indeed—
Himself—in his old habit—his old self—
What! back again, Clotaldo, for a while
To swear me this for truth, and afterwards
All for a dreaming lie?

CLO.
Awake or dreaming,
Down with that sword, and down these traitors theirs,
Drawn in rebellion 'gainst their Sovereign.

SEG. (about to strike).
Traitor! Traitor yourself!—
But soft—soft—soft!—

You told me, not so very long ago,
Awake or dreaming—I forget—my brain
Is not so clear about it—but I know
One test you gave me to discern between,
Which mad and dreaming people cannot master;
Or if the dreamer could, so best secure
A comfortable waking—Was't not so?
(To Rosaura).
Needs not your intercession now, you see,
As in the dream before—
Clotaldo, rough old nurse and tutor too
That only traitor wert, to me if true—
Give him his sword; set him on a fresh horse;
Conduct him safely through my rebel force;
And so God speed him to his sovereign's side!
Give me your hand; and whether all awake
Or all a-dreaming, ride, Clotaldo, ride—
Dream-swift—for fear we dreams should overtake.

(A Battle may be supposed to take place; after which)

ACT IV

SCENE I.—A wooded pass near the field of battle: drums, trumpets, firing, etc. Cries of 'God save Basilio! Segismund,' etc.

(Enter Fife, running.)

FIFE.
God save them both, and save them all! say I!—
Oh—what hot work!—Whichever way one turns
The whistling bullet at one's ears—I've drifted
Far from my mad young—master—whom I saw
Tossing upon the very crest of battle,
Beside the Prince—God save her first of all!
With all my heart I say and pray—and so
Commend her to His keeping—bang!—bang!—bang!
And for myself—scarce worth His thinking of—
I'll see what I can do to save myself
Behind this rock, until the storm blows over.

(Skirmishes, shouts, firing, etc. After some time enter King Basilio,
Astolfo, and Clotaldo)

KING.
The day is lost!

AST.
Do not despair—the rebels—

KING.
Alas! the vanquish'd only are the rebels.

CLOTALDO.
Ev'n if this battle lost us, 'tis but one
Gain'd on their side, if you not lost in it;
Another moment and too late: at once
Take horse, and to the capital, my liege,
Where in some safe and holy sanctuary
Save Poland in your person.

AST.
Be persuaded:
You know your son: have tasted of his temper;
At his first onset threatening unprovoked
The crime predicted for his last and worst.
How whetted now with such a taste of blood,
And thus far conquest!

KING.
Ay, and how he fought!
Oh how he fought, Astolfo; ranks of men
Falling as swathes of grass before the mower;
I could but pause to gaze at him, although,
Like the pale horseman of the Apocalypse,
Each moment brought him nearer—Yet I say,
I could but pause and gaze on him, and pray

Poland had such a warrior for her king.

AST.
The cry of triumph on the other side
Gains ground upon us here—there's but a moment
For you, my liege, to do, for me to speak,
Who back must to the field, and what man may
Do, to retrieve the fortune of the day.
(Firing.)

FIFE (falling forward, shot).
Oh, Lord, have mercy on me.

KING.
What a shriek—
Oh, some poor creature wounded in a cause
Perhaps not worth the loss of one poor life!—
So young too—and no soldier—

FIFE.
A poor lad,
Who choosing play at hide and seek with death,
Just hid where death just came to look for him;
For there's no place, I think, can keep him out,
Once he's his eye upon you. All grows dark—
You glitter finely too—Well—we are dreaming
But when the bullet's off—Heaven save the mark!
So tell my mister—mastress—
(Dies.)

KING.
Oh God! How this poor creature's ignorance
Confounds our so-call'd wisdom! Even now

When death has stopt his lips, the wound through which
His soul went out, still with its bloody tongue
Preaching how vain our struggle against fate!

(Voices within).
After them! After them! This way! This way!
The day is ours—Down with Basilio, etc.

AST.
Fly, sir—

KING.
And slave-like flying not out-ride
The fate which better like a King abide!
(Enter Segismund, Rosaura, Soldiers, etc.)

SEG.
Where is the King?

KING (prostrating himself).
Behold him,—by this late
Anticipation of resistless fate,
Thus underneath your feet his golden crown,
And the white head that wears it, laying down,
His fond resistance hope to expiate.

SEG.
Princes and warriors of Poland—you
That stare on this unnatural sight aghast,
Listen to one who, Heaven-inspired to do
What in its secret wisdom Heaven forecast,
By that same Heaven instructed prophet-wise
To justify the present in the past.

What in the sapphire volume of the skies
Is writ by God's own finger misleads none,
But him whose vain and misinstructed eyes,
They mock with misinterpretation,
Or who, mistaking what he rightly read,
Ill commentary makes, or misapplies
Thinking to shirk or thwart it. Which has done
The wisdom of this venerable head;
Who, well provided with the secret key
To that gold alphabet, himself made me,
Himself, I say, the savage he fore-read
Fate somehow should be charged with; nipp'd the growth
Of better nature in constraint and sloth,
That only bring to bear the seed of wrong
And turn'd the stream to fury whose out-burst
Had kept his lawful channel uncoerced,
And fertilized the land he flow'd along.
Then like to some unskilful duellist,
Who having over-reached himself pushing too hard
His foe, or but a moment off his guard—
What odds, when Fate is one's antagonist!—
Nay, more, this royal father, self-dismay'd
At having Fate against himself array'd,
Upon himself the very sword he knew
Should wound him, down upon his bosom drew,
That might well handled, well have wrought; or, kept
Undrawn, have harmless in the scabbard slept.
But Fate shall not by human force be broke,
Nor foil'd by human feint; the Secret learn'd
Against the scholar by that master turn'd
Who to himself reserves the master-stroke.
Witness whereof this venerable Age,
Thrice crown'd as Sire, and Sovereign, and Sage,

Down to the very dust dishonour'd by
The very means he tempted to defy The irresistible. And shall not I,
Till now the mere dumb instrument that wrought
The battle Fate has with my father fought,
Now the mere mouth-piece of its victory
Oh, shall not I, the champions' sword laid down,
Be yet more shamed to wear the teacher's gown,
And, blushing at the part I had to play,
Down where that honour'd head I was to lay
By this more just submission of my own,
The treason Fate has forced on me atone?

KING.
Oh, Segismund, in whom I see indeed,
Out of the ashes of my self-extinction
A better self revive; if not beneath
Your feet, beneath your better wisdom bow'd,
The Sovereignty of Poland I resign,
With this its golden symbol; which if thus
Saved with its silver head inviolate,
Shall nevermore be subject to decline;
But when the head that it alights on now
Falls honour'd by the very foe that must,
As all things mortal, lay it in the dust,
Shall star-like shift to his successor's brow.
(Shouts, trumpets, etc. God save King Segismund!)

SEG.
For what remains—
As for my own, so for my people's peace,
Astolfo's and Estrella's plighted hands
I disunite, and taking hers to mine,

His to one yet more dearly his resign.
(Shouts, etc. God save Estrella,
Queen of Poland!)

SEG (to Clotaldo).
You
That with unflinching duty to your King,
Till countermanded by the mightier Power,
Have held your Prince a captive in the tower,
Henceforth as strictly guard him on the throne
No less my people's keeper than my own.
You stare upon me all, amazed to hear
The word of civil justice from such lips
As never yet seem'd tuned to such discourse.
But listen—In that same enchanted tower,
Not long ago I learn'd it from a dream
Expounded by this ancient prophet here;
And which he told me, should it come again,
How I should bear myself beneath it; not
As then with angry passion all on fire,
Arguing and making a distemper'd soul;
But ev'n with justice, mercy, self-control,
As if the dream I walk'd in were no dream,
And conscience one day to account for it.
A dream it was in which I thought myself,
And you that hail'd me now then hail'd me King,
In a brave palace that was all my own,
Within, and all without it, mine; until,
Drunk with excess of majesty and pride,
Methought I tower'd so high and swell'd so wide,
That of myself I burst the glittering bubble,
That my ambition had about me blown,
And all again was darkness. Such a dream

As this in which I may be walking now;
Dispensing solemn justice to you shadows,
Who make believe to listen; but anon,
With all your glittering arms and equipage,
King, princes, captains, warriors, plume and steel,
Ay, ev'n with all your airy theatre,
May flit into the air you seem to rend
With acclamation, leaving me to wake
In the dark tower; or dreaming that I wake
From this that waking is; or this and that
Both waking or both dreaming; such a doubt
Confounds and clouds our mortal life about.
And, whether wake or dreaming, this I know,
How dream-wise human glories come and go;
Whose momentary tenure not to break,
Walking as one who knows he soon may wake,
So fairly carry the full cup, so well
Disorder'd insolence and passion quell,
That there be nothing after to upbraid
Dreamer or doer in the part he play'd,
Whether To-morrow's dawn shall break the spell,
Or the Last Trumpet of the eternal Day,
When Dreaming with the Night shall pass away.

(Exeunt.)

NOTES

www.ingramcontent.com/pod-product-compliance
Lightning Source LLC
LaVergne TN
LVHW101925220826
846093LV00009B/368

* 9 7 8 9 3 9 1 5 6 0 5 0 8 *